Heart
OF THE
Ache

BELLIS SANTOS

PAGE PUBLISHING, INC.
Conneaut Lake, PA

First originally published by Page Publishing 2021

ISBN 978-1-6624-1987-4 (pbk)
ISBN 978-1-6624-1988-1 (digital)

Printed in the United States of America

Just say goodbye.

Remembering

You are always on my mind.
I wish, sometimes, love was not blind.
Remembering our times make me smile.
I wish you were still a part of my lifestyle.

I miss you now that
We do not see each other often.
The kiss you stole from my lips
Still has me stunned.

I miss you.
I miss your touch.
I crave it.
My skin aches for it.
It remembers.

Responsible

My mind doesn't go blank. Not at all—it moves, it thinks, it burns.
What if I never allowed you in?
What if I never let you come near me?
Would it have been different?
Would it have been a good idea?
Would it have saved me the ache, the pain, and the humiliation?
Would you have been different?
Would you have married me in the end?

All these bottled up feelings coming out after two years
And you're responsible.
I blame you for my uncertainty
But I cannot blame you entirely.
It was my fault for letting you in,
It was my fault for thinking it was okay,
It was my fault thinking you would change, believing your empty
        promises.

You are the cause of my bleeding heart,
My shattered mind,
And my fright of losing the friends I have now.
The walls that had been rebuilt
You took down only to hurt me.
You were the wolf in disguise,
That I saw coming and believed could be tamed.
I reached out my hand only for you to bite me.
My scars,
My wounds,
My shattered heart...
For all these, I hold you responsible.

Regret

What if we never liked each other?
What if we never met?
Would not meeting you take the pain away?
Would not dating you save me from all the pain and aches?
My only regret is not stopping it before it got out of hand.

Ugly

It's like breathing air underwater,
Or breathing without lungs,
Living without a heart,
Smiling with tears,
And I can't escape this feeling.

Every smile is crucial,
Every cry is a "scream for attention,"
As a child I was told to "grow up,"
Now as an adult, I am not allowed.

My live is a facade—
It's become a facade,
I don't know what is real and what is not,
My darkest thoughts tell me the good things are not real,
They tell me I am not worth it,
And I believe it.

My negative thoughts cloud my judgment
And every smile, every tear,
I wonder if it is really what I am feeling,
Do I really feel sad?
Do I just want attention?
But then again, what is wrong with that?

What is wrong with wanting someone to ask if you are okay?
What is wrong with being a little selfish?
What is wrong with not wanting to feel alone?
Why do I not trust anyone with these feelings?
Why can I not come out with it?

Oh, because I am supposed to be happy all the time,
Because no one can know how dark I get,
Because they will run away,
They will push me away,
I should only be what they know me as.

The one who smiles,
The one who is loud,
The one who fights,
The one who laughs,
The one who can make anyone happy.

But who will make me smile?
Who will make me laugh?
Who will be there for me when I am down?
Because it feels like no one ever is.

It feels like no one cares,
No one is ever there,
And I do not like being alone,
I do not like what is underneath.
I do not like that is really me,
I do not like the girl beneath:
The smiles,
The laughs,
The shouts,
The jokes.

I do not like what is underneath,
Because that is when the facade fades
And the ugly comes out.

Underneath the facade is the ugly.
The ugly I conceal,
The ugly no one knows about,
The ugly that controls me,

The ugly that pushes all away,
The ugly I cannot talk to anyone about,
The ugly my parents ignore,
The ugly I cannot ignore,
The ugly I do not want my friends to know,
The ugly I wish someone would come to ease,
The ugly I wish I had someone to go to about,
The ugly I wish someone would see.

But in the end—
Underneath the facade—
It is just the ugliness and me,
Loneliness and me:
The ugly I cannot get rid of.

The Cellar

She is evil.
We have been together since I was a kid,
She tells me I am not worth it,
She makes me believe it is true,
She is strong—too strong.

I can't ever fight back,
It is never physical, always psychological;
She knows where to hit where it hurts.
She comes for me
When I am vulnerable
I cannot hide—not ever;
Not from her.

The cellar is dark
And I am trapped.
I am supposed to be the one holding the key,
I am supposed to be the one in control,
I am supposed to be the one that is strong,
I am supposed to be able to control her.

When I am in front of the mirror,
I see her behind me, judging,
And slowly, my mind turns dark.
The light cannot go through—no—
The light cannot reach.
And I get trapped again.

Again in the cellar,
Again in the dark,
Alone again;

And she is looking down on me again,
She is mad,
Mad at the world,
Mad at me,
Angry with me,
Furious with me.

Angry I do not fight back,
Angry I am worthless,
Angry I am nothing,
Angry that
She is looking down
At herself.

I had the keys all along
With me,
Next to me,
On me;
I just refused to use them.

I am angry I cannot break free from my own cage,
I am angry I am weak,
Angry that I lock myself in,
Angry that even with the key,
I will not try to break free—
Try to get out.
Out of the cellar of my mind.

The Mind

There is no air,
Nothing moves,
Nothing around,
Lonely.

There is a void,
Something is missing,
And the darkness
Doesn't clear.

The clock stopped
A while back—
Too far back
To remember when.

Time and time again,
Light would hit,
Not frequently, but enough,
Just enough for her to
Have the strength to fight
Against the dark once again.

Today

The world today does not hold the same meaning as before,
Promises are no longer kept,
Love is no longer true,
And hate guides the mind in this life.

Sadly, this is today,
The "now" everyone wishes to live in—
What a disgrace.

Series

I
I did not let anyone else in
So that I would not get hurt.
I think it is funny that
You wormed your way into my heart
Only to break it again.

II
Why did you leave me?
Was I so unbearable?
I hate you the most.

III
Being ignored is the most uncomfortable silence anyone can be in.

IV
You were the first and the last
Person to ever get to see my heart.
Because the day you left
Was the day it dissolved into oblivion.

I'm Trying

"You can't wear that."
"It's not you."
"Make a choice."
"That's not the right one."
"Why don't you fight for what you want?"
"Don't speak to me like that. I'm your mom."
"Talk to me. I will listen."
"Why are you acting childish?"
"How much do you have left to pay on your credit?"
"Wow, that's a lot. You have a lot of money to spend."
"Grow up!"

I'm trying.

Fire Turned Ice

The sun was bright today,
Beautiful, calming, no dismay.
There was a dog out alone,
And it was so cute we had to take him to a safe place—one he can
own.

It was all smiles and laughs,
I even forgot my past.
We were making dinner outside,
There was absolutely no downside.

But when the night came,
That's when the facade faded.
It was time to get rid of it,
It could no longer in my closet sit.

The fire was going low,
And when I started to feed it, it grew.
The papers went up in flames,
And once in the fire, it could no longer be reclaimed.

The things of yours wound up in flames,
And though it was supposed to help me heal,
It only made me feel like everything around me was surreal.

My heart ached watching them burn,
And my eyes began to water.
The fire made my heart yearn,
It made my stomach churn.
I didn't like letting you go,
I didn't like watching you burn,

It made my heart turn cold, ache
As the fire—the monster ate it all.

The flames flickered, snapped, and danced,
Like it knew I would not go in and reach for them,
Like it was taunting me,
Haunting me.

The hardest part wasn't letting you go,
The hardest part
Was making my heart turn cold—
Break—again,
As I watched helplessly
As the fire that consumed you.

A part of me broke tonight,
A part of me wanted you to hold me tight,
The song came on—
The one that torments me endlessly,
The one we were supposed to get married to,
The one we both cared for.
I couldn't help falling in love with you,
You were the fire,
You always will be
While I used to be.

Now there's not even a spark,
I can't bring myself to try to.
You were the fire,
You were the one that could make me spark,
But just like the flame you are,
You burned me to a crisp.

Today you were the fire in the pit,
And I was the paper getting tossed in.
Now the fire is out,

Just like you and I,
I may have been cold, lonely, and put out,
But even the coldest hearts have feelings—
A reason to how they became that way.

We were like a flame,
The flame was combined once
But then consumed.
For a short period of time, we were like that,
But then, I turned to ice,
And you—the flame—consumed it all.

You _____

You said you loved me,
You said you cared.

You promised me the world,
You promised me you'd be true.

You swore you'd marry me,
You swore our love was undying.

You vowed you loved me more than the sun loved the moon,
You vowed you loved me more than the moon loved the stars.

You told me we either live together or die together,
You told me I was worth it.

You *liar*.

It Bothers Me

Your perfect smile,
It made me go wild;
It bothered me.

Your hand in mine,
It felt so kind;
It bothered me.

When our love died,
I cried;
It bothered me.

The promises we made,
They meant nothing to you in the end;
It bothered me.

In 2017,
The year was bleak;
It bothered me.

When you moved on,
The hope I had switched off;
It bothered me.

I still care for you,
But you didn't pursue;
And it bothers me.

The Painting on the Wall

It reminds me of the pain,
The pain that is constantly hidden.
It torments me at times
Because it does not age like I do.
It sits there frozen in space,
And I cannot tell which would be best.

To live in a world where time is frozen?
Or to realize you feel the same as an unmoving, unaging, unreal painting,
Or, perhaps, to wish life was nothing more than a canvas,
To wish life was more than just a painting on a wall.

Having someone captivate such complex emotions;
I wish there was someone I can share my pain with
Besides just painting a canvas,
Because she just stares at me
My creation, my painting on the wall.
She does not understand she was created through pain,
She only knows that she is in pain,
And I am the reason for it.
She will never understand it,
Just like me.

Just like me,
The painting on the wall stays forever in one place,
Unmoving,
Alone,
Nonexistent to the world.

The Painting on the Wall II

Each stroke is seen,
The colors—dark and lonely.
The more people look, they pretend to see—
To understand.

People can look at her all day,
But they will never understand the dismay.
Amateur work they might say,
But what is amateur in feeling?
Is feeling considered amateur?

Is pain and loneliness wrong?
Is it supposed to be a feeling I am not supposed to express?
But how can the painting on the wall change that?
How can I change myself?
The painting on the wall was created.
The judgment upon her felt like acid.

She cannot change how she feels
Because that was how I created her,
Because she is just a painting on the wall;
She can never heal,
I guess that is the difference between her and I.
I can change, she cannot.
I can rearrange, she cannot.
I can do plenty of things while she cannot,
But it would all be for naught
For we both feel the same:

Lame, lonely, desolate, isolated, alone…
And just like her, I cannot change it
Though I wish I could.

Enough

My goodbye to you on the twenty-fourth
Was the hardest thing for me to do.
Henceforth,
I will forget you, but not out of the blue.

It will take time for me to heal,
But my time with you won't be completely forgotten.
I just wish this scar was easier to seal,
For now, the memories will be shunned.

Saying goodbye—how can I describe it?
It was like the flutter of wings, consistent.
The whoosh of the breeze, cold.
A pebble in a shoe, uncomfortable.
An uncharted island, lonely.
A life without meaning, bleak.
A world without colors, colorless.

You didn't understand my love for you,
But it was not like it mattered
Because it was not enough to make you stay.
Losing you was heartbreaking,
Losing you was like a part of me being stripped away,
I was not enough to make you stay.

But you see,
I am not sorry
Because I was enough.
I was,
Whether you thought so or not,
If you had to even think that way,

Then perhaps you weren't enough for me.
You gave up,
You weren't worthy,
But *I* was enough.

Losing you will always cause me pain,
But nothing can compare to the heartache you caused me
When you decided *I* wasn't worth it.

You were my greatest hello,
You are my hardest goodbye.
My heart is at ease I decided to let you go,
I will watch as time goes by
Because I made it through hell and back.
I will live the highlight of my life
Though, what is left of my halo is black.
I've learned through the strife,
And I will never again fall for your bluff.
That made me feel I was not
Enough.

The Dragon

I watched as the dragon's fire rippled in the air, crinkled even,
He mocked my misery, knowing I must feed it in order to stay alive,
Else, my mind, it will wreak havoc,
Amuck.

The dragon breathed out its petrifying fire,
Burning the tips of my fingers, reminding me it must be fed;
I feed it cautiously,
As his red flame rises from the pit of his stomach,
Ready to blow out wildly.

But I held my hand out to it,
Ready to feed the beast,
In my hand, my sacrifice to it,
And just then, its fire ceased to feast,
I watched helplessly,
And I felt ghastly
As I watched in a daze
As his fire took everything from me;
The dragon scrutinized me,
Knowing I could do nothing to save my sacrifice form it.

But what it did not know: they were pieces—
Traces of me,
My letters to him,
Pictures of us…
Dissolved to ashes:
The dragon consumed it all,
The fire pit burned it all,
And *I* threw it in.
I sacrificed the toxic pieces of me away,

Now I just feel a bit astray,
But soon it will all dissipate.

For now, my heart is heavy,
And my mind is in spirals,
To get better I pray,
I need strength to get through the trials,
I wish to end this game of life at times
Because the dragon is in the back of my mind.
Soon the dragon will have no effect over my feelings,
Shortly, I will stand among the kings,
In time, my heart will no longer feel like the ravines.

The dragon may have burned my pieces,
But I will stand above the ashes,
And I will no longer let the past cause my heart anymore gouges,
The dragon may have the traces of my past,
But not the pieces of my future.

Series

V

Silence is the darkness of lonely.

VI

The strongest triumph alone,
But that does not mean they want to be.

VII

I'm tired,
Tired of the screams in my head.

VIII

I may be here,
But my mind wanders
With thoughts of the past.

IX

We had so much chemistry
Every time we were together we ignited,
But we also burned.

Not Anywhere

I do not wish to go anywhere.
Not inside,
Not outside,
Not about,
Not around,
Not over here,
Not over there,
Not anywhere.

I do not wish so speak to anyone.
Not in my house,
Not at the meetings,
Not around town,
Not through social medias,
Do not even call.

But, I do not wish to be alone.
Not in my room,
Not in the house,
Not over here,
Not anywhere.

This Morning

This morning was fine,
I even had time to dine.

I woke up confused,
But my sleep was not abused.

I studied at 4:00 a.m.,
But at the meeting I could not comment.

My energy was drained,
I could not even smile.

I no longer wish to be alive,
The feeling is consuming me inside.

This feeling I cannot eliminate,
But this morning, I was fine.

I'm Tired

5/20

I'm tired of the weight,
I'm tired of the responsibilities,
I'm tired of doing things wrong,
I'm tired of trying to please people,
I am tired.

For once I want to please myself,
I want to make myself happy,
Or just go missing,
I wanted to be cared for.

I'm tired of being strong,
I'm tired of not being able to level up,
I am so exhausted.
I don't want to continue like this,
But I can't say how I feel.

I'm tired of being a disappointment,
I'm tired of being here,
I'm tired of being me,
I'm tired of being a witness.
No one cares for me,
No one texts me,
No one holds me,
No one tells me the truth,
No one can stand me.
I've suffered alone for too long,
I don't know if I can take much more,

I'm not important here or there,
I'm tired of not meeting anyone's expectations.

I'm tired of living,
I'm tired of being the failure,
I'm tired of being me,
I'm tired of me;
I am *tired*.

That Once Was There

I remember when I sparked,
I was a flame that couldn't be contained.
My fire was warmth,
My fire was comfort,
My fire was *me*.

I was free like the wind,
Grand like the ocean,
Wild like the savannah,
Merry like the hyena,
Mysterious like the moon,
My mind extended to the sky,
My knowledge extensive like the ocean floor;
I remember when my fire *burned*.

But alas, like all great things,
Time ruins them,
And the people that once were,
Are now gone;
A ghost in a shell,
Where if an eye you were able to behold;
You would see a spark that once was there.

A spark they remember about,
But do not know how to ignite,
The flare now nothing but a spark,
Not on nor off,
A flickering flare,
Slowly fading to nothing.

Cleansing

I watch as the rain falls.
It bounces off the broken Buick in the backyard,
Waters the plants planted on the ground,
And creates noise that calms the mind.

The rain washes away any essence of nature,
The mud,
The leaves,
The birds in need of a bath...

But no matter how long I stand under it,
The rain does not seem to wash me away.

I'm Sorry

I stooped so low,
I wanted to go,
I had hit my lowest point,
And I am sorry,
This time,
I won't disappoint.

Silence

I regret keeping quiet,
I regret not telling you,
I regret the times I was told to be silent,
I do not regret the times we shared,
But most of all,
I regret not being able to be myself.

Silence II

I was ashamed of who I was,
I was afraid of letting go,
I was kept quiet often,
And I stayed quiet because that was what I knew.

Now, at twenty three, I still do,
I feel like a child that is not allowed to speak,
And I feel like a puppet when I do.

There are days when my bottled emotions break loose,
And everyone does not know what to do,
Yet I cannot say what I feel,
Because it is so unnatural for me to do so.

It will take time for me to learn,
Because when I finally break,
I say things—
Hurtful things.
Maybe because I was kept silent
Is the reason I am blunt,
People do not need to hear what I say,
But that does not give them the right
To keep me silent.
No one has that right.

Once

Her eyes twinkled,
Once.
Her entrance drew attention,
Once.
Her laugh boomed in a crowd,
Once.
Her presence stirred the assembly,
Once.

Once,
Her soul was a *blazing* fire,
She shone as bright as the sun in the sky,
She was the pillar of light at night,
She was the path to peace,
And she was pleasant and kind…
Once.

The girl that once was
Is no longer,
But she is trying to live
Like she once did,
To be wild—to survive
The world she was deprived of.

Because once,
A long time ago,
She had not met him,
He who caused this loss,
Both were to blame,
He for depriving her youth,
And she for not living after the fact,

She was brave,
She was happy,
Once, upon a time.

Live

Live your life to the fullest,
Be free, but cautious,
Fall in love, but know your worth,
Be the best friend you've always wanted,
Have a plan,
If it doesn't go the way you wanted,
Think of it as a detour,
Get to your destination,
Follow your dreams,
Reach your goals,
Forget the past,
Learn from your mistakes,
Live.

For the Broken Hearts

We have died today,
Left to wither and wilt,
We have turned brown—
Our soul gray,
Our hearts have split.

Though your heart has broken,
Know you are not alone,
Go out in the sun,
Or go to the lake and throw a stone,
Because you stun.

No man deserves your tears,
No one deserves to see you broken,
It will be hard to face the fears,
But know you have won.

You did not lose him,
He lost *you*,
Though your days may feel grim,
Don't bottle your feelings of him.

Scream and cry and whine,
Do whatever you want to heal,
But don't spend your time to come wallowing over that swine,
Remember, you have friends that will help you through your ordeal.

5/16

On 5/16, I wanted to scream.
I wanted to disappear into oblivion,
I wanted someone to hold me,
I wanted the rain to wash me away.

I fell into despair that day.
My throat burned with unshed tears,
My mind wandered endlessly with my fears,
I wanted to leave,
I wanted to die.

On 5/16, I broke.
I wanted to go to the beach,
I wanted to swim,
I wanted to *YELL*!
I WANTED TO *YELL* AT THE WORLD!
SCREAM UNTIL I COULDN'T ANYMORE!
I wanted someone to *hold* me.

It was so cold that day
And I was so numb.
The rain was pleasant—
I bathed in it.

I stood under the pouring rain alone,
The cold tickled my skin.
I couldn't cry,
I couldn't scream,
I couldn't breathe.

My feet were so red,
My clothes were drenched
As I ran around,
I kicked the ground,
I screamed internally.

On 5/16, I broke,
And *no one* was there to see it.

Not Once

A Letter to Mother

"I don't like being at the house," I say.
Not once was I asked why.
Not once was I a matter of importance to you,
At least, that's how I felt.
I cannot speak out without you reasoning it is time for me to move
    out,
But not once was I asked why,
Not once was I asked why I do not like being at the house.

Because we never see eye to eye,
Because we do not like the same things,
Because there is constant arguing,
Because you make me feel like I am not good enough,
Because everyone sees me,
But no one see's my suffering.
I can cry out such as I did now and it will only result into another
    fight.

On how I am unappreciative,
On how I do what I want,
On how I am ruining my life,
On how I am just never enough.
You tell me how you can no longer stand me,
That you have to endure.
But you fail to see that you are the same way.
I have to deal with you too.

I am in my room because I know the moment I step out,

I will get in trouble, just by even looking at you.
You said you didn't want to go out in the morning;
You should have just canceled.
Maybe then we wouldn't have fought.
I can't go to you about anything and you don't care.
You've told me before that you find it hard to love me.
That's why I never want to be home.
I know where I am not wanted. I can feel it.

And as you read, you're probably getting angry and probably annoyed.
Or perhaps you just ripped this letter to shreds without even opening it.
For once, just listen to me because this will be the last time I ever go
    to you for anything.
Just listen and don't speak.
Everyone tells me that I need to speak about my pain, and yet no one
    ever wants to listen.

You're supposed to be there for when I need you.
You say you're afraid to talk to me.
I don't believe you because you always chose the most random
    moments to tell me off.
You're not afraid to ruin my mood.
You're not afraid to hurt my feelings.
So no, you're not afraid of me…

You just gave up on me.
Just like everyone else.
You were just always quick to judge.
But not once did you ever ask me why.

Not *once*.

Internally

It's those days that get you.
When you don't want to be holed up anywhere.
You just want to go out and scream.
No, it was more intense than that.
My mind was heavy with thoughts, but at the same time, it was
   blank.

My voice was stuck in my throat, but I could talk.
My body was paralyzed, but it was moving like normal.
I felt lonely, yet I was surrounded by my friends.
I was angry and upset, but I was smiling.
I was calm, but I was anxious.
My heart was frozen, but it was beating.
I was crying and screaming and kicking and yelling, but no one heard
   me.
Inside, I broke, and no one saw.

Stop

I don't want to be strong anymore,
I want to give up.

I want this world to end,
And I don't ever want it to come back.

I want it all to just...stop.

Do You?

I lay awake at night thinking of what went wrong,
Do you?
My memory haunts me with words said and promises unkept,
Does yours?
I remember the days we laughed all night,
Do you?
I miss the feeling we used to have,
Do you?
You're still in my heart,
Am I?
I love you,
Do you?

Goodbye, My Love

I got closure today.
6/13 will be always remembered,
The storm came at bay,
And the past went away,
My emotions once at rage
Has now been upstaged,
My anger is now at peace,
My eyes no longer cry,
My heart no longer aches,
My mind wanders to the teenage dream we were caught in.

We were amazing,
We were fun,
We were wild,
We loved,
There were times you made me feel amazing,
There were times when you were amazing.

The car brought back the good old times,
Back when we smiled,
Back when we danced,
Back when nothing else mattered,
Back when we were kids,
And I realize I still love you,
Two years and I love you,
But I also love me.
Finally letting you go
Will bring me back,
And I'm scared,
Scared of losing you,
Scared of starting over.

I'll never forget us,
I'll never forget the way you made me feel,
How you made me soar,
You weren't the one that got away,
You were the one that set me free,
Goodbye, my love.

Party Girl

I love dancing,
I love being surrounded by friends,
I love the music that plays;
It makes my feet move,
But I am not a party girl.

I can doll up,
I can be dancing in my seat,
I can show signs I'm not with anyone,
But I still don't get asked to dance.

I hate parties,
I always feel alone,
The men are just talking amongst themselves in a corner,
Or dancing with their partner,
Or out asking every pretty girl out there to dance,
So not me.

Parties make me feel so ugly,
My friends are out on the dance floor
While I warm my seat.
It's always just me and the married women;
I watch as their husbands come and ask them to dance,
And I wish I had someone too.
I'm not wild,
Or crazy,
You'd find me alone,
Sitting in the corner,
Wishing to be:
A party girl.

Presently

There was a time
When I was kind.

Once,
I got along with everyone.

At a time,
Scholarly, I was exceptional.

Before,
I had motivation.

Long ago,
People came to hear me.

In the past,
People *wanted* to hear me.

What surprises me the most
Is that I haven't changed much.

But now,
People have long forgotten me.

At the moment,
I have little to talk about.

Presently,
No one wishes to listen.

has shriveled up.

I now,

onely girl,
g in the car

he parking lot
marina.

irl who has lost
erything about herself.

Me

Lately, things haven't been okay.
I feel like my life is going away,
Slipping though my fingers,
Slowly getting further and further away.

But I have a goal,
And I hope it will help me feel
Like I am going somewhere
Though, I don't have support.

I'm used to doing things on my own,
But sometimes I wish I wasn't so independent,
I wish I wasn't so alone,
I wish I was anyone but me.

When

He was strong—fierce.
He was a lion—filled with might.
His smile warmed hearts,
His hands calloused,
And the difference was,
He is mine—
I mean *was*.

I remember when he was only strong for me,
When he was a lion for me,
When he only smiled for me,
When his calloused hands only held me.

He was everything to me.
I remember when his texts brightened my day,
When he could come over,
When he would make excuses to come over.

But just as quick,
He became a ghost to me.
His texts became less and less,
And he stopped coming over.
His excuses to why became more and more.

I knew something was wrong,
But nothing was said,
Nothing was spoken,
And I drifted.
I drifted offshore
And the waves,
Oh, how they swept me under.

The water,
How it drowned me.
Then I grew gills: submitted;
And it was hard to swim back to shore: reality
Because I was abandoned.

My pride broken,
My dignity shattered,
My heart turned cold,
And I was forgotten within the waters,
Left to drown in my own tears.

While lost in the water,
You were no longer in my mind,
Nor in my memories,
You became a dream,
But you never left my heart.

It remembers
When you made it soar,
When you made it beat,
When you were there.

Ice Queen

The tale of the Ice Queen—behold,
A tale long forgotten, a tale untold!

She was once a woman pure and sterling,
But now a woman with blackened feeling.

Never was a power so strong as she,
For cursed she be.

Roaming her kingdom with frozen suffering,
She keeps to her aching.

For the tale of the Ice Queen is this—behold!
To be forever ice cold.

A woman whose past cannot be put behind—
Her future a blur.

And she will forever remain that way:
Isolated and in decay.

Because this is the tale of the Ice Queen—behold
Cursing herself will always keep her heart cold.

Causing thyself pain
Gives invisible bloodstains.

And that is the tale of the Ice Queen—behold,
To forever keep *herself* cold.

Secrets

There was an untold story,
Twinkling in her eyes.

One that would take
A lifetime to unravel.

Series

X

Why do you fear the stars?
Because their magical gleam
Illuminates my scars.

XI

It's heavy inside,
Though we do not acknowledge
This is loneliness.

XII

Despair in the dark of night,
The voices in the mind do not silence,
Your eyes closed, but seeing everything.
Every night, I lay awake,
Waiting for my time to rest my anxieties.

XIII

The sky was on fire—
Bright, and lovely, and lively
In the dream, she was.

Sea of Secrets

Her mouth held big smiles,
Humorous laughter,
Clumsy mannerisms,
And a loud presence,
But the sea of secrets
Her eyes held;
No one would ever know.

Questions

Remember when we first met?
We laughed like crazy didn't we?
Or how about those crazy sleepovers?
When we told secrets late at night, remember?

They were good times, weren't they?
Yeah, you were the best.
But I have to know, did I hurt your knife?
You know, when you stabbed me in the back?

Did you clean it up?
Washed and put it away?
Like nothing ever happened?
Did you even look back at the times we had?
Or have you forgotten already?
How you killed our friendship?

Demons

There were two of them.
She was peaceful, happy even,
While he caused nothing
But mayhem.

She was kind and witty
While he was rude and angry.

She tried her best to survive,
Though she was confined and deprived.

He would be the only one who thrived,
The only one who was alive.

As time went on,
She grew weak and alone.

And he took control,
As he stole her soul.

And she slowly died
Because I decided
To feed my anger
Instead of her.

Night Sky

Her essence was like the night sky,
She was a canvas for anyone to just *use*.

Comets came and went,
Keeping her company for a short period of time.

The stars glowed and clustered together,
Leaving her to yearn.

And as the moon,
She was scarred.

When the sun came up to see her,
She slowly hid away.

Because she was not
Used to the light.

Beginning

Things never start fair,
And we cannot say we don't care.

The beginning was harsh,
Perhaps we were in a marsh.

Waterlogged,
Deeply slogged.

The water was dark;
It was thick.

The more we searched for air,
The more we were ensnared.

And we began to sink,
No matter how hard we kicked.

We could not break through the surface,
And it became aimless.

We let ourselves go down—
Drown.

Life became a hoodwink;
Goals no longer in sync.

And the beginning suddenly
Became the ending.

About the Author

Bellis Santos is a book loving, poet writer, and fiction author. When not obsessing over the latest book she can be found posting her latest chapters of her fiction stories online. Born and raised in California, Santos uses her skills to help those around her.

CPSIA information can be obtained
at www.ICGtesting.com
Printed in the USA
BVHW081332010721
610979BV00005B/171